Poems for the Common Man

By David Weese

Copyright © 2008 by David Weese

ISBN No. 978-0-578-00219-4

All poems were written by David Weese and all pictures were taken by David Weese (except where noted). All rights reserved. No portion of this book may be reproduced or copied in any form or by any mechanical or electronic means without the specific written permission of the author, except by a reviewer, who may quote brief passages in their review. Layouts/page editing by David Weese. All rights reserved.

Poems for the Common Man

If you're looking for lofty, elitist poems that are nearly impossible to understand, this is not the book for you. But if you are looking for easy to grasp poems that will touch you, move you, bring you understanding and maybe even a little healing, - welcome home.

This book is dedicated to my wife Debi, who has nurtured and encouraged my poetic career in many ways, from reading countless revisions to being awakened in the middle of the night to read my latest piece, to being the inspiration for many of my poems.

This is also dedicated to Joy Burki Watson, whose guidance and friendship has been crucial. Thanks Sis!

The profits from this book will be donated to:
The National Coalition For The Homeless

Table of Contents

Title	Page
A Poets Prayer	6
Love and the Swallow	8
Because	10
Find Me There	12
Instrument	14
Challenger/Discovery	16
Flor d' Luna	18
Jewel of the Mountains	20
Hold On, Beloved One	22
Ever and Onward	24
Wanderers	26
Photograph	28
For Debi	30
Daughter of the Dawn	32
Silenced	34
Dear Thom	36
Flying Fortress	38
A Christmas Promise	40
Mountain Wildflower	42
In the Deep of the Night	44
Fourth of July	46
The Chosen One	48
In Case She Forgets	50
October Eyes	52
To Make a Difference	54
The Gift	56
Cold Walk	58
On Letting Go	60
The Willow	62
Feather in the Wind	64
The Lion	66
Empty Cup - Finding You	68
Crystal	70

Table of Contents

Title	Page
Fingers of the Wind	*72*
The Stones	*74*
Citadel	*76*
Pearl	*78*
For a Fighter - For David	*80*
Winter's Chill	*82*
The Weaver	*84*
The River	*86*
Flowergarden	*88*
Seamstress	*90*
Looking For You	*92*
Simple Light	*94*
Rollin' Down to Dixie	*96*
Willow	*98*
Memories	*100*
Hearts	*102*
Vows	*104*
Castle's Call	*106*
Silver, Blue and Gold	*108*
Love Ain't Easy	*110*
Full Circle	*112*
Footprints	*114*
Songbird	*116*
Mother Earth	*118*
Echoes of Legends	*120*
Approaching Darkness	*122*
For Gale	*124*
The Column and the Ivy	*126*
Yesterday's Girl	*128*
Searching for the River	*130*
Still Yourself	*132*
Grandfather Mandela	*136*
The Ice Prince	*138*

A Poet's Prayer

Come ...
take up the pen
the little voice says

And we ...
will weave magic

Misty, the path beckons
and I follow
gentle ...
dewy green ...
down into the hollow
to the wellspring ...
whose source I know not

But on it flows

It has touched a few
may it touch many

May it stand alone
... apart from me

Gateway to Heaven

Love and the Swallow

As a swallow
love wheels and dives above you

Seeming touchable in its antics
But elusive ...
as lightning
it bursts asunder

Leaving only
ashes ...
dust ...
Falling thru singed fingers

spiraling down ...
like snowflakes

Obscuring in a whitewash blanket
the earthy sorrow
the clingy moss of pain

We reach for an illusion
spinning free on glorified wings
... a teasing dance on thin air

So far from mother earth
from her love of the will
from her swallow

Diving ...

Cavorting ...

*But always heeding
the gentle beckon*

*Of mother earth ...
of her reality
of her fruits*

*Reach ...
Touch ...
Fly ...*

Because

*Long ...
has been our journey*

*And many ...
have been the travails*

*The path ...
sometimes obscured
sometimes bathed ...
in sunlight resplendent*

*Lost ...
have I been
in life's wilderness*

*But follow ...
will I
where her love leads*

*Seek ...
will I
her sunlit paths*

Because ...

*Her touch ...
soft as moonlight
... dancing across the waters*

*Her voice ...
cool as morning-mist
... nestled in the hollows*

*Her embrace
... my solace*

my deliverance

Her smile
... my light
my salvation

Her love
... my way back home

Author's Notes: Happy 25th anniversary babe.

Find Me There

Find me
in the high mountain
wildflower
My fragile beauty grows
stubbornly ...
on savage heights
My simple splendor
persists ...
despite the blizzard's lash

Find me there

Find me
in the rocky mountain
stream
My gurgling laughter
soothes the most troubled,
lonely spirits
My cool waters
restores the most parched,
desolate souls

Find me there

Find me
in the sweeping mountain
vista
My splendid majesty
speaks of my faithfulness
My timeless beauty
speaks of my everlastings

Find me there

Find me
in the steely-eyed bear
My finely tuned senses
keenly aware
of all that surrounds me
My awesome strength
fearlessly treads
the darkest forests

Find me there

I am ...
your high tundra
wildflower
your delicate
yet persistent beauty
when all around
is pain

I am ...
your gently tumbling beck
your tranquil
healing laughter
when all around is turmoil

I am ...
your stalwart massive
your solid rock
when all around is
crumbling

I am ...
your bear

your guardian angel
when all around is terror

I walk beside you
like the bear
unseen in deep forests
yet all powerful

I nurture you
strengthen you
teach you
... in mysterious ways

I cherish you
chasten you
as my child
... because you are

I knew you and loved you
before you were born
I bring you comfort
in your departing

gently gathering you
homeward

I am
the alpha
the omega
the beginning
the end

I am ...
the master
the creator
the healer

I am ...
your closest confidant
your Heavenly Father
your loving God

... Find me

Author's notes: For Michelle

Instrument

The masters loving hands
crafted it only from the finest

It's acoustics ...
it's resonance ...
almost magical

What beauty ...
what joy it could bring

Yet the gift
stands idly in the corner

Strings rusty
... out of tune

Treasure ...
as if lost to antiquity

Oh, great giver of gifts ...
I give it back

I have mislaid your magic
in dusty corners

I have disguised your beauty
in this earthly veil

Take this gift ...
this instrument ...
this pen ...
and play it

play me

Author's Notes: About the gift of writing, and my tendency to neglect it.

His Instrument

Challenger - Discovery

T minus 9 ... 8 ... 7 ...
We have main engine start

Your fetters explode away
and from your bowels is unleashed
seven million foot-pounds of fury
setting you free from the surly bonds of earth

If our wills could have made you fly
that day ...
you would have soared
into that inky, midnight blue ...
to bring home our wayward ones
to fly with their spirits ...
to emblazon their names upon the heavens

Ellsion ...
Christa ...
the rest of you dear friends
We have returned

We feel your presence
we fly with your spirits
we are one with your purpose

Old glory ...
she's come a stormin' back

... speed, 3600 feet per second
... altitude, seven nautical miles
... nine nautical miles downrange

Discovery ...
Go with throttle up

Go with throttle up
Roger Houston
... throttle up
... all systems nominal

Author's notes: Written the day Discovery returned to space after the Challenger tragedy

Photo courtesy of NASA images

Flor d' Luna

Rarest prize ...
softest jewel

And yet
my heart ...
cannot express it

My soul ...
cannot fathom it

She is ...
the vision
that sees me
that heals me

She is ...
the hope
of my soul
... welling up unto everlastings

She is ...
my smile
in the rain ...
in the pouring rain

She is ...
my rarest treasure

... my flower of the moon

Authors Notes: Inspired by a Santana song of the same name. Happy 15th anniversary babe.

Unfathomable Beauty

Jewel of the Mountains

Many happy seasons
have I passed
meandering your soaring heights

And still ...
your wonders
fail me not

Your love ...
has been my pass
through these foreboding ranges

Your direction
... my path
through this desolate wilderness

Your strength
... like a storm
raging over the distant peaks

Your purpose
... stalwart
as the snow swept craggy heights

You bring me comfort
as a cool, piney forest
in the noonday heat

You give me hope
as a eagle
soaring over distant peaks

Mysterious you are
as a misty morning meadow
bespeckled with dew

Beautiful you are
as the wildflower
high on the mountainside

Your smile
… dappled sunlight
filtering through the aspens

Your laughter
a babbling brook
tumbling through the valley

Your tears
… precious
as glistening gems of morning dew

Your embrace
beckons as soft moonlight
reflected o'er a high mountain lake

Ever …
will I wander your valleys
enraptured by your vistas

Ever …
will I slumber in your meadows
content in your bounty

Author's Notes: Happy 20th anniversary babe

Hold On, Beloved One

The more I know
the less I understand

This life ...
it's so hard to know

Things come our way
... suddenly
... painfully

Yet this life
She is of balance

She calls home
both the young
and the old
... and at her choosing

Things we love
are just taken away
... unfairly
perhaps ...
even unjustly

The answers
... elusive
perhaps ...
for the next life

We ask
to know the mind of God

But the question
is of balance

For what life takes
She also gives back

She gives pain
so we can know love

She gives us death
so we can know new life

She
is of balance
Her ways
are of love ...
are of wisdom

Yet wisdom ...
sometimes hard earned

So walk ...
my beloved one
walk out of this darkness
... walk to the light

Her ways
are of balance
The dawn
always breaks

Author's Notes: For my daughter on the loss of Elmo and Delilah

Sunlight's Magic

Ever and Onward

Each day
reveals more
of you ...
of me

Each day
brings more

wonder ...
peace ...
strength ...

With you ...
I have seen
many seasons

With you ...
I would spend
many more

The succor you grant me
envelopes my senses

everlasting enticements
are what drive me on

And all of my seasons ...
all the rest of my seasons

I would spend
enraptured in you

Everlasting Strength

Wanderers

*First of December
first snow too
… only stuck on the grass*

*Night falls
…temp drops
…wind kicks up
panes rattle furiously*

*Climbing down into a cold bed
I get that old chill
… and remember*

*That chill…
meant I was warming
… the violent shivering was over*

*"Picked a good spot tonight
… no wind*

*Might be three …
maybe four days
…till someone figures out
I've been sleeping here"*

*Oh, people …
our children wander the streets*

... wind kicks up
... temp drops

Where do they go?
Where ...
do they go?

Author's Notes: This one reveals a very painful part of my past, but it's an experience I wouldn't trade for the world. It taught me compassion.

Photograph

Found you yesterday

... back of the drawer
... kinda tattered

that youthful face
those angry eyes

But there you were
staring back at me
as if ...
from another life

How my heart ached
for you

Aye ... young man
and the things
I could tell you

The things you think you know
... you don't

Harshly ...
life will teach you
You will learn
and you will change

Your trusting heart
- a mile wide
she will crush it
and you will change

And oh ...
my altruistic young lad

Greed ...
will rob you
Evil ...
will visit you
and you will change

Pain ...
will be your bedfellow
Sadness ...
will follow your days
and you will change

But across those years
stare those eyes
- still full of fire

Aye ... old man
and the things I must tell you

and how my heart aches
for you

For you ...
have changed

The man
that stands before me

... I know not
This man
has forgotten who he was

That altruistic young man
... he has changed
... he has gone

His dreams ...
changed
Now ...
long forgotten

His passion ...
changed
Now ...
fallen by the wayside

His pain ...
changed
Now ...
oft' self inflicted

We ...
were going to make a
difference

We ...
were going to find a way
to make 'em see

Old man ...
Tell me -
you really haven't changed

Tell me -
you really haven't
hardened your heart

Tell me -
you really haven't
closed that door

Author's Notes: Written after finding the only known picture I have of myself taken while I was on the streets.

The "Photograph"

For Debi

A gentle voice
beckons me waken

A soft manner
breathes life
into me ...
into this dreary day

Does she know?
and how do I tell her?

She is my purpose ...
my reason why

Satin caresses
silky, bedded kisses
lacy surrender ...
and I am complete

Does she know?
and how do I tell her?

Only her completeness ...
truly calms my fears

Come ...
take my hand
we will wander down the years

Be my purpose
Be my reason
in this madness

All else had faded

There is ...
only you

Nature's Perfection

Daughter of the Dawn

The little things
- soft in manner
do not leave you

Earth beauty
Daughter of the dawn

Your heart
showers me with goodness

Your loving simplicity
is easy to grasp
... hard to let go

It is your quiet times
that move me

In your slumber
I find peace

In your peace
I find purpose
I find a beacon

Dear daughter of the dawn
Forever shine your light

And I ...
will follow it home

Author's Notes: For my wife

Dawn's Magnificence

Silenced

*Stand
and struggle
to drink her in*

*Yet she ...
simply overwhelms*

*The grandeur
of her stony heights
... her flower-strewn slopes
tumbling down
to waters
sometimes lashed
sometimes caressed
by cold mountain winds*

*- eagles' shrill cry
echoes across the valley
- deer move
through cool pine forests*

*Man stands awed ...
humbled ...
to complete silence
struck dumb ...
in this splendor*

*Insignificant
he stands
in this wilderness*

... a mere speck

Here ...
the rule of man
no longer applies

Here ...
the laws are as ancient
as time herself

Here ...
We are just sojourners

Mother Nature ...
simply allows us to pass
in grateful silence

Dear Thom

The rivers ...
are fordable

Through the mountains ...
there is a pass

No one said it would be easy

Dawn ...
will always break
We must accept
the gift she brings

Time ...
is her gift

Her cool waters ...
eventually restore
The pain ...
eventually subsides

Life is sweet
... drink it in

The lady of the morning
adorns herself each day
in new raiment

Author's Notes: For a friend who was struggling.

Natures's Cool, Healing Waters

Flying Fortress

Locals would count them going out
... lumbering off into the gloom
and again as they'd limp home

Many hundreds ...
fell to the Madman

But again and again
they would rise up
and deliver
... medicine for the Madman

The Rhineland
the Ruhr
over Berlin herself
They broke the back of the Madman

Not many left now ...
these machines you helped breath life into
... made you misty when you saw one

You were our Flying Fortress
a bastion of stability
when the Madmen would rail

You would rise up
again and again
and deliver
wisdom, courage
When none else was to be found

So wing away
my Flying Fortress ...
my steel eagle

You have left your mark
You will be missed

Author's Notes: In memory of my favorite uncle,
Richard Wesley Bell

A Christmas Promise

Cinnamon smiles
and gingerbread kisses
Twinkling light magic
in anticipating little eyes

Gently, mother earths' snowflakes
bedeck the earth
Her subtle masterpiece
a gift
sent to soften hearts
... to remind us

She is peace

Yet there is no peace

Hate abounds
under winters' simple majesties
Calloused greed thrives
amid her silent splendor

Her gift, a reminder
... a promise of new life
She is unerring faithfulness
in a world torn with strife

Her methods
oft' harsh
And so too our world

Yet her ways are of balance
Strife ...
brings meaning to peace

So sleep little ones
Dream sugar plum dreams
of jolly old fat men
and sleighs on the roof

You are part of her promise
You have opened my eyes
To peace oft' unnoticed
To the richness of life

Mountain Wildflower
In Memory of Linda Cale

Tiny
Simple

Yet ...
so lovely

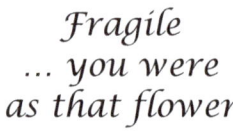

Fragile
... you were
as that flower

Yet stubbornly
you grew
where you should not

One just wanted
... to gather you up
... to hold you
... to protect you

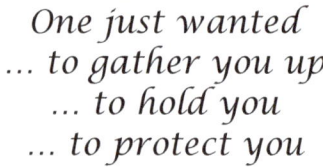

But protect you
I could not

Shelter offered
was not taken

Winters' winds
you would face alone

Oh girl ...

How I miss

your simple beauty

*... delicate flower
with the radiant smile*

~ ~ ~

*Were you with us
in those mountains?*

*Did you drive
that storm away?*

~ ~ ~

*It is that flower
I will remember*

*the one that grew
where it should not*

*I will forget
those fallen petals*

*... claimed
by the cruel frost*

Author's Notes: I know poetry should not need an explanation, but this one was a personal gift to the family. Linda was the one of sweetest, kindest people I've ever known. Plagued with physical problems, she could smile through it all. Unfortunately, Linda fell in with the wrong crowd, and though I tried to help her, sadly, her death was drug related. She passed away while we were vacationing in Colorado. Many tears were shed writing this poem.

In the Deep of the Night

There is a little boy
in a time ...
in a place ...

known only to memories
... and the wind

Deep ...
in his feverish night
that little boy
called forth magic ...
with a word

... Mama

And that gentle magic
was there ...

That soft voice
that cool hand ...
on forehead
and cheek

It would be better soon

Ah ... how the years have flown

But there is still ...
a little boy

who craves
that gentle magic
that sweet ...
cool ...
soft ...
healing voice
in the deep of his night

... It will be better soon

Thank you, Mama

Fourth of July

Just a local thing ...

High school marching band
Fire trucks all shined up
... sirens wailing
Lions Club float
Fat caddy's
carrying even fatter politicians

Then it was the WWII vets
... banner flying

Then Korea
... marching crisply

Straggling along behind
you came

Kinda' rag tag
just shufflin' along

No banner
no proud men
no crisp march

These were our boys
who'd risked it all

The cane - the wheelchair
told the story

And I ...
was ashamed
I put my hands together

I clapped loud

*The people stared
then they too
felt my shame
and I was not clapping alone*

*You could almost see the chins come up
... the chests swell out
The cane
bore less weight*

*Welcome home, boys
We were wrong*

*Stand tall and march
We were wrong*

*Author's Notes: This is a true story written after attending a
hometown 4th of July parade*

The Chosen One

And where does she go
when the rains come?

Where does her heart
find refuge
when the rain
falls in her soul?

Oh, friend ...
take heart

For everything ...
there is a reason

For every tear
... a smile

For every lonely night
... the promise of a new
dawn

God sends us nothing
we cannot endure

Yet sometimes His gifts
are obscured in our tears

God gave you another
who also needs
a place to go ...
when the rains come

A place of refuge ...
from the storms of life

A rock ...
in which to shelter his soul

God ...
makes no mistakes

He chose you
for a reason

He gave you loneliness ...
so you could know his

He gave you pain ...
so you could give comfort

He gave you tears ...
so you could dry his

Oh, friend ...
dry your tears ...
open your eyes

You were chosen
in His wisdom

As for everything
there is a reason

"Like a father pitieth his children, so the Lord pitieth them who fear him. For He knoweth our frame. He remembereth that we are dust." Ps. 103, 13-14.
For a special friend who is raising an autistic child.

Tranquil Waters

In Case She Forgets

And she lays there
covers ...
securely tucked under her chin

Moonlight caresses
soft hair and cheek

Touch her
and she stirs

sweet recognition
... in my darkness

Her soft sigh
... softer voice
reaches deep inside me

Lover ...
the images you bring me
... are timeless

I am old ...
and you are with me
and my heart is full

My days ...
golden

My life ...
complete

Come ...
I will take you
and hold you

*And speak to you
words of everlasting*

*I will know no joy ...
but to die in your arms*

* * * *

"Whither thou goest, I will go .... And thy people, shall be my people..." Ruth 1, 16.

October Eyes

Gently
dawn creeps across his
pillow
Usually met with disdain
but today
... anticipation
They would be coming
and he would be ready

His usual rounds
forgotten today
He would be there
when they came

Strategically placed on
the porch
the old wooden friend
would rock him into
remembering

Spinning idly down
the leaves remind him
of their youth
of his seasons

How they loved
to frolic in those leaves
And how their merriment
would warm his heart

Today -
he was four-score and ten
His winter -
approaching

Just short miles away
surely they would come
today

But the hours ...
dissolve away
October's long light
now his only companion

Finally a message
... more a whimper
is left

Please wake me when
they come

Now teardrops
and moonbeams
mingle patchwork on the
pillow

Silent sorrow
shared only
with the silvery face in
the heavens

Wake me when they come

Please ...
Wake me when they come

Author's notes: The true story of a man in a nursing home who's kids never bothered to visit him on his 90th birthday.

Fading Light

To Make A Difference

To not understand
forces working within

To be given something
... never asked for

To feel driven
by a gift
not always understood

To know
the right words
can make a difference

Things
touch you differently

The joy
brings tears
The sadness
leaves slowly
Others' pain
becomes your own

And all
because this gift
... because this pen
can make a difference

Oh, great giver of gifts
I strive
yet I fail

Help me earn the right
to wield this pen
... to make a difference

Solitary Heights

The Gift

How do I portray
the gifts she gives me
the love she sends me

And she comes to me
... and smiles
and it all falls away

For in her eyes
glow sweet everlastings

In her arms
lies solace unfathomed

She is ...
my morningstar
my evensong

My quiet hope
in the still of the night

Restless I lay
and dawn overtakes me

I have received ...
more than given

As a man
imperfect ...
I am

As a man
a debtor ...
I am

A gift
to repay
I have not

So ...
I will give
as I have

I give ...
myself
in all that I have
in all that I am

Yet more ...
I owe
and still more

For she is ...
my morningstar
my evensong

my quiet hope
in the still of the night

Author's notes: Happy 10th anniversary babe

Misty Mountain Magic

Cold Walk

Yesterday I saw you ...
alone on the corner

- bag too heavy
- coat too thin.
- street too busy
- eyes in the distance
on your cold walk home

You paint a sad picture of us all

There is so much sorrow
yet we close our hearts ...
and hide our eyes ...
and just pass by

"There are no easy answers," we say
"There is only so much one can do"

So we do nothing

What can be done ...
must be done

We cannot just drift by
and blow the chance
to place that little ball of warmth
in the pocket of someone
on their cold walk home

Snowbound Passages

On Letting Go

Seems just yesterday
you were learning to walk

Today ...
the training wheels came off

And you ...
fly away

I reach to "steady you"
... knew you didn't need it
... guess I'm just reaching
'cause I want the time back
'cause it's hard to let go

The time ...
slips thru your fingers
... melts away
Thank God for the pictures

Such a precious gift
yet we see the instance
and miss the moment

We fret the brush strokes
never seeing
the masterpiece unfolding

Seize the time ...
drink deeply of its sweet nectar
pour yourself into their springtime

For the season is fleeting

A Captured Moment

The Willow

And from where
will she draw her
strength

The storm
is upon her

Her boughs
... tossed about
on the winds of change

Her branches
... stripped bare
by the gale's assault

Her head bowed
... by pain
not her making

But nature
has her ways

Her healing
oft' comes slowly

Those leaves
so cruelly stripped away

she will restore
in her season

And those boughs
she designed
to bend ...
but not break

Weep ...
you may

But restore you
she will

At your feet
tumbles a stream

Sent your way
by the healer of hearts

It's cool waters
will bring healing

It's gentle laughter
will make you whole

But only
if you reach out your
roots
and drink it in

It is your winter
your time of sorrow

But your spring
will come

Your leaves ...
your beauty
will return

Her healing waters
will strengthen you

will restore you
will make you whole

All things ...
in her season

Author's Notes: For my friend Cassandra.

Feather in the Wind

Ever ...
will we remember you

That mischievous smile
that twinkle in your eyes

That warm kitchen
... that warmer heart

Yet shortly before dawn
you chose
to steal away from us

You took flight
like a feather ...
in the wind

So steal away
to that place of rest

Away ...
from the travails
of this life
Away ...
from the afflictions
of this earth

On ...
to a better place
where tears ...
are forgotten
where pain ...
is no more

*So steal away
Steal away homeward*

*Home …
where loved ones
await you*

*But ever…
will we remember
that mischievous smile
that warm heart
that feather…
in the wind*

*Forever imprinted
… on our lives
… on our hearts
… on our souls*

Author's Notes: In loving memory of Evelyn Jacob

The Lion

A Cherokee
Strong ...
Proud ...

One who had not forgotten the old way

Found in his lore was this:
Hold your head high
... be somebody

But remember ...
life is not fair

He was my lion
powerful ...
cunning

Yet a gentle hand pointed the way

He was found in backyard wrestling matches
In the early morning mists on a favorite bass hole
In boyhood memories of his terrifying heroics
In jaunts off together in the crisp fall air

And could he roar ...

But now
my lion ...
has fallen asleep ...
and will roar no longer

*So sleep ...
my father ...
my lion
For the cycle is complete*

Your legacy is not forgotten

*Your seed lives ...
and is strong ...
and roars*

Author's notes: Written for a friend who lost his father.

Empty Cup - Finding You

EMPTY CUP

There is a hole
a hole in a little heart

Someone has stolen away

Gone beyond
and left an empty place
an empty cup
held in pitiful little hands

Where are you now?
Why have you gone?

How I long to have
known your touch
just the simple pleasure of
your presence

Nothing brings comfort
No one could replace you

If I could have you back
for just one day

Papa ...
we'd go sailing

FINDING YOU

Such a forlorn little
figure
kneeling there in the
grass

Looking so small ...
so lost ...
in the well intentioned lies

"I could have known him
but I have been cheated
by good intentions

"I brought roses
He loved them
... how did I know?

"My tears have fallen on
your grave as a warm
spring rain
I have brought the roses

"Oh papa, I have found you
I have found you"

And it read:
A loving husband and
daddy

Oh, ... my beloved little one

The warm sun
shines down upon you
May it bring you
understanding

The gentle wind
caresses your hair
May it bring you peace

Author's notes: My wife's parents split up when she was just an infant, and through unfortunate circumstances she never really got to meet her father. Then when she was 12, he died suddenly from a brain aneurysm. After we were married, I set about to find him. Not only did I find his grave, I found her half-brother, and just short weeks later, we were able to attend his wedding.

Crystal

Glowing clearer
... is my love

It was
radiant ...
yet refracted ...
as through crystal

Today ...
it became
pure ...
unadulterated ...
light

It is ...
that warmth
that radiance

As in your face
after ...

Where would I go?
And what would I do
without your pure ...
priceless ...
light?

I think I saw a man dying today

God ...
how I treasure your light

Author's Notes: Written after passing a tragic accident.

Crystalline Waters

Fingers of the Wind
For Christopher

Ever
will I remember you

My friend
once my brother

Many happy hours
I whiled away with you

On my bike
you were that kid
I never could quite catch

You were always
a few lengths in the lead

The fingers of the wind
playing in your
auburn hair
as if in defiance, saying -
"Catch me if you can"

How the time flies
How things change

Our lives
just went separate ways

There was a time
when no one was closer

There was a time
when your voice
on the other end of

that phone
was my salvation

When I needed you
I knew you'd be there

And now
I am here for you
my friend

Yet I come
With a heart
full of sorrow

and questions
forever unanswered

But never
my friend
... never
will I forget you

You will always be

that voice -
on the other end of
the phone

that friend -
that would help me if
he could

that kid -

I never could quite catch

flying ahead ...
in the lead ...

with the fingers of the wind
playing in your auburn hair

Author's notes: In memory of one of my best friends, Chris Malone, who passed away of natural causes at far to young an age.
Chris was one of the few people who tried to help me when I was on the streets.
Miss ya' Chris.

The Stones

Saw you...
four days before

Found out ...
four months later

Simple affair
... hurried and hushed
Family only
... private tears

A chariot of iron ...
on ribbons of steel
gathered you homeward

- There was a collection
for the stone

Your stone ...
a white powder
... made you blind to the chariot

Now the stones ...

lie in the arms ...
of mother earth

... could have pulled the reins in
... jerked him up short

But instead ...
I was part of the collection
... for the stone
that took him down

Author's notes: In memory of Jack C. This poem is a very painful one for me, as it is an admission of my failing a friend - completely and totally. He became involved with drugs, and I did nothing to stop him. I just walked away from him. Later, I found out that he gotten too high, and accidentally stepped out in front of a train. It still haunts me to this day.

In the Balance

Citadel

Their vision
spanned a lifetime

Together …
they would build it
this place of refuge
safe, as in the Fathers
hands

* * *

For love …
she is like water

The tranquility
of her quiet waters
soothes the stormiest of
souls

The beauty
of her thundering
cataracts
reshapes the earth

faithfully wearing away
all that will not last

revealing the foundation
stones
with which this citadel
would be built

stones …
that would stand
the test of time

* * *

Long and arduous
would be this labor
with many perils and
travails

Yet the vision
… persisted

Stone by stone
would they build it
following the impeccable
plans
laid by the master
architect

And now the vision
has become reality

Their citadel stands
stalwart and secure …
among the craggy heights

This labor of a lifetime
stands illuminated
in the golden light of His
love

Behold it now
in the long light of sunset

*Built
in the Masters ultimate design*

*beautiful
... beyond compare*

Author's notes: Read at the celebration of my parent's 50th anniversary. Congratulations Mom and Dad. An incredible achievement; something that makes me proud of you both.

Pearl

Mother nature ...
she has her ways

Take her oyster
gnarled ...
algae covered ...
unsightly

But nature ...
she has her ways

Her secrets ...
her magic ...
she hides away

I looked
and saw beauty

Hidden
in a shell

But nature ...
she has her ways

All that is needed
is the shucker's knife
held in deft hands
... her hands

A gentle twist reveals
the rich luster
of mother of pearl

Beauty ...
making the gnarled
seem insignificant
The other side
reveals the truth

But deeper still
hides her masterpiece
... hides her pearl

it's glow
rarer ...
cooler ...
softer than moonlight

It's shape
perfect ...
beyond compare

never needing
the cutters wheel

Mother nature ...
she has her ways

You ...
are that oyster

And within you
hides that pearl

Find it girl
... find it

Mother nature ...
she has her ways

Her secrets ...
her beauty ...
she hides away

Author's notes: Written for a young lady struggling mightily with self-doubt. Sometimes seeing our own inner beauty is all we need to come to believe in ourselves.

For a Fighter - For David

A tear of frustration
falls on my shoulder
Your day - soon over
The sandman beckons

All I can do is hold you
... and long to tell you
of your miraculous beginning
... of the inferno that was your cradle

On a stormy spring night
you came to us
Three months early ...
barely a pound

Your odds
... slim

Yet to you ...
odds meant nothing
You just knew to fight
... and win

If I could just make you understand
You are so strong

This really doesn't matter
You are so strong

Author's notes: My son was born three months early, and weighed 1 lb. 4 1/2 oz. at birth. Just 12 1/2 inches long, I could hold him in one hand. But God was kind. David Jr. defied all the odds and somehow pulled through. Every time I look at him, I have to realize that he is a stone-cold miracle. This was written when he was about 2.

His Wonders Never Cease

Winter's Chill

A bundle of fur
and hot garlic breath
Wriggling energy
and sloppy dog kisses

Out run me on my bike
... ya' could
... little legs just a churnin'

We grew together
We were friends

Your friendship ...
simplistic ...
yet fantastically beautiful

To you ...
nothing ever mattered
We were friends

But the years
and the winter's chill
... have come

And today ...
Dad found you
... sleeping

Author's notes: Written in memory of a dog I had as a boy.
Miss ya' Nappy

Sparkling Memories

The Weaver
Silver Thread- Subtle Hands

Woven ...
by the Master's subtle
hands

A single silver thread
was wound
through the tapestries
of two lives

Born ...
of innocence
and the silver-lined
memories
only childhood love can
bring

Somehow this thread
remained unbroken
as two lives
took separate paths

Lines of communication
remained open
sustained ...
by subtle hands

That silver thread of love
was never forgotten
... skillfully woven
into the fabric of two
lives

Down winding roads
the Weaver takes us

Through the refiner's fire
sometimes
He must lead us

Yet He never forgets
that silver thread
now lovingly entwined
in the tapestries
of two lives
now become one

Walk now
in His silver-lined
sunshine

your tapestries
... woven together
in His time

your love
... rekindled
in His season

your silver thread
... rejoined
with His blessing

As with mine

Author's notes: Read at my cousin Bonnie and her husband Charlie's wedding reception on 8/12/06

Photo courtesy of Bonnie McCallister
Taken on a stream that feeds the Ocoee River, the place where Charlie proposed to Bonnie

The River

And they have heard
her call
Her gentle voice
whispers of love and
devotion ...
echoing unto forever

And we will gather
this day
And they
will begin this journey

They will become
... wayfarers
on this river ...
this lady
from which life
her very self
emanates

That gentle brook
gurgling ...
rushing
ever on -
on to meet herself

The ageless one
the timeless one

Giver of gifts
... of life
... of quiet solace
... of peace

Her way
is of patience ...
is of faithfulness
gently tumbling over
stones
that once were mountains

And they say
She and I
bid you join us
bid you join our love

We will swear
before Heaven and Earth

We entreat you dear ones
... carry us to the river

But the river ...
she is wiser that we

These vows
now sweet words
... expressions of rapture
will one day
be tried by fire
... word for word

And they know these
things

and they will do it
... still

They will swear these oaths
before friends
before family
before Heaven
before Earth

Love ...
counteth not cost

Wise is she
... the river

Learn her ways

She moves mountains ...
with unrelenting patience

And is she not
truly the essence of
faithfulness

Learn of her ...

Friends of water
shall withstand
trial by fire

Author's notes: Read at the wedding of my sister-in-law, Julie & her husband Jon on 7/13/1996

Flowergarden

*It is spring
and you are young*

*Yet today ...
briefly ...
I glimpsed your summer*

*Dazzling ...
resplendent glory
that autumn will not fade*

*Yet I am charged
to be your gardener*

*to tend beauty
not always understood*

*to cause to flourish
things I do not know*

*Still ...
I am willing*

*Allow your beauty
to open my eyes*

*Permit your petals ...
blossoming in the spring rain
to open my heart*

*It is spring
natures' time for teaching*

*Teach me
I am still young*

Author's notes: For my daughter Cassandra.

Captured Innocence

Seamstress

Why God calls some
unto the deep
at the moments he does
is a question
only for the Heavenly
Father

He does so
... in his season
... in his wisdom
beyond
our understanding

Perhaps ...
her work was done

~ ~ ~

As a seamstress
lovingly ...
she stitched together
the fabric ...
of many lives

Stitches that nurtured
children ...
grandchildren ...
great-grandchildren

Her deft ...
gentle stitches
crafted the fabric
... forming the very life
of a family

Crafted ...
with a love
that was honest
and unfailingly accepting

A love ...
that was simple
and yet ...
so profound

So sleep ...
beloved one

... Sleep

Your gentle legacy ...
has touched us all

Those magical stitches
you lovingly sewed
throughout our lives

Forever will remain
a guiding light
... for us all

A light ...
ever ...
beckoning us homeward

Authors's notes: In memory of Joyce Jacob, my wife's aunt.

Heavenly Light

Looking For You

These eyes
have seen the years
... seen the fears
... seen the tears

With the knowledge of the ancient
and the wisdom of a young fool

With a heart made of gold
yet a heart made of stone

I am ...
who I would not be
I would be ...
what I am not

Yesterday
I went looking
to find you
... but found me

These eyes
searched for you everywhere
and found you nowhere
- yet found you everywhere

These eyes ...
saw a new love
for you ...
my little wanderer

Author's Notes: This is about the first time my son turned up missing. The thoughts that went through my head as I searched the neighborhood for him were literally life-altering.

Paths to Distant Places

Simple Light
In memory of Roddy Weese

Light
pure ...
simple ...
radiant ...
light

It shone from you
it was you
... it was your essence

Life
for you ...
was so much simpler

You lived ...
here among us
and yet ...
you lived with the angels

Your love
... unconditional

Your nature
... gentleness

Your understanding
... simple
yet hard to fathom

With you
nothing ever mattered
... friends
true and blue

When we met
instantly ...
you loved me

Years past
and we met again
and still ...
you loved me

Still ...
that same
warm ...
wet ...
wonderful ...
love

that same
simple ...
warm ...
wonderful ...
light

Simple?
and how ...
did I learn so much?

Light
... you were
shining into many lives

Pure ...
simple ...
radiant ...
light

So return ...
beloved one

Return ...
from whence you came

Return ...
to perfection

Return ...
to the angels

Return ...
to the Light

Author's notes: My cousin Roddy was born with a profound case of Downs Syndrome. I doubt his vocabulary ever reached 200 words. But the one thing my uncle was told shortly after he was born, and always repeated, was that people with this disability seem "to live with the angels." If you've ever known someone with Downs, you'll know what I'm talking about. Their's is a simpler, much more beautiful world.

Rollin' Down to Dixie
In memory of George Weese

As the road rolls up
before me
my mind drifts back ...

On an August day
many years ago
a child is born
to a proud ...
persistent ...
yet fragile man

The child
- imperfect

Yet God
is so wise

Plans that we make
seldom fit his design

He saw ...
a diamond in the rough

He saw ...
the right man
at the right time

God would use
that imperfect child
to gentle ...
to refine ...
this fragile man
into a force

This man
would make it better
for all imperfect children

A man
never stands so tall
as when he stoops
to help a child

And this man
stood so tall

And so today
I'm wending my way
through the Tennessee
hills
and the red Georgia clay

- rollin' down to Dixie

Uncle ...
I'm on my way

Author's notes: This poem is a follow on to "Simple Light" on the previous page. George was Roddy's father. Roddy was 54 when he died, but when he was born, the only options for my Aunt and Uncle were to institutionalize Roddy or keep him home and try to educate him on their own. Special education just didn't exist back then.

My uncle was pivotal in getting the South Carolina and Georgia legislatures to provide funding to educate special needs children.

Uncle George was somewhat of a contradiction in terms. A very fragile man emotionally, he could be an absolute lion when it came to things like pushing this legislation or in business matters.

But my Aunt and Uncle's one wish was that they outlive Roddy, as he required such intense care, and there was simply nobody who could care for him the way they could. Thankfully, my Uncle outlived him by two years.

There was a delay in getting the word to me, but when I found out George passed away, I was determined to make his funeral.

I wound up driving 910 miles - straight through - from Chicago to Augusta, Georgia, arriving at 1:30 in the morning to attend his funeral at 10:00 that morning. That's just the kind of man my Uncle George was.

Willow

And I know not
save that I am here

Weeping
... the years
... the fears
The painful things
that have come before

Neptune ...
has spewed forth his fury
Thor ...
has railed against me

And I know not
... and I know not how
save that I am here
... and that there is a
reason

And the pain
... the emptiness
it calls me
yet I know not where
save that I am here
and I know not why

But I know
there is a reason
... for this pen

And I know not ...

save that it is here

This pen ...
is like the brook
that wends its way past
my feet

She laughs ...
and trips over stones
and gurgles merrily
beneath me

She ...
is the cool water
that restores me

And I know not ...
save that I
would be your willow

I would bend
... and weep
... and write

So you ...
will not break

And I know not ...

save that I am here

Cool, Restoring Waters

Memories

Ticket stubs
... a ride thru yesteryear

Pressed flowers
... from faded glory days

Love letters
... pages tired from reading

Tattered pictures
beauty ...
frozen in time

That ring
- it wore thin with time

Treasured nothings
relics ...
some from pain's distant haunts

And the memories
put aside ...
but never forgotten

Faded Glory

Hearts

*It is in these dark times ...
that I need her most*

*See it ...
she will ...
maybe in time*

*For now ...
all I have
is what I have*

*But even ...
as it is
I give it ...
I give it all*

*To offer ...
I have only myself*

*To tide the gulf
I have only truth*

*Shine your light
your pure ...
unadulterated ...
light*

*And they say
"Love knows hidden paths"*

*and amongst them
... find me*

for long have I sought you

*Life's battle
... have I waged*

*Only for ...
that confluence of hearts*

*Only for ...
that love I hold
a treasure
... so rare*

Vows

For better or for worse
... easily said

But the reality?
Often ...
we're not ready to pay that price

A lifetime ...
is a lifetime
... and not one day shorter

A commitment of marriage
... is just one day longer

We forget
what we vowed
and remember what we envisioned

Two ...
become one

But had we envisioned
the price of this union?

Did we see
that we can no longer be our own?

Vows do not unite
two into one

two must compromise
... and change

*two must work
... and give
... and give up
... and give again*

*And then ...
maybe ...
if there is love enough*

Castle's Call

*In peril ...
nevermore shall she be
For I ...
have hidden away her heart*

*Stolen it away ...
deep in the castle's keep
within my soul*

*Forever ...
will her name
ring in my halls*

*Forever ...
will her charms
warm my frostiest hearth*

*Ever ...
will she be mine
and ever ...
will I be hers*

*Forever ...
will her name
stir my soul*

*Forever ...
will she be ...
my fair and gentle maiden
my damsel in distress*

*An oath to thee, fair maiden:
Whisper only my name
I will hearken ...
and draw nigh*

Queller of fears ...
Am I
Slayer of dragons ...
Binder of wounds ...
I would be

Forever ...
Will I be your Galahad
Forever ...
Will I hide your heart
high ...
in these lofty towers
hidden ...
in the secret passageways
deep ...
within the castle's keep
that is my soul

Forever ...
fair maiden
Will I hide thee there

A knights oath
forever have ye ...
fair maiden

A knights oath

Author's notes: Written for the wedding of my brother and sister-in-law Ed and Rose.

Silver, Blue and Gold

Silver...
is for devotion
... shining pure

Hear loves call...
hear the gentle whispers of forever

Blue
... is for the rain

For trial's sunless oceans
... for toil's windswept distances

Yet, in the midst of the storms
a masterpiece of purpose was wrought

Gold...
is that masterpiece
... that hard fought prize of the faithful

standing...
radiant against the dawn

Treasure of a lifetime...
now hangs timeless

silver...
blue and gold

... in the halls of forever

Author's notes: Written for the 50th anniversary of my wife's grandparents, Clarence and Evelyn Jacob.

Timeless Treasure

Love Ain't Easy

So often we let our emotions fool us

"I just don't feel that old feeling
Where is that romantic spark?
Surely the thing is dying"

Oh friend ...
take heart

Love is not an emotion
It is an action ...
a decision of the will

Emotions are as the wind
they will change
they must

The distant days will come

But with patient
... day by day
decisions of the will

also come the close days

For how can there be closeness
... without distance

How can there be joy
... without sorrow

View to Forever

Full Circle

Weep not for me
for I
the weary wayfarer
have found sojourn
in the promised land

I have found peace
across that great river

Weep not for me
for I
have been full circle
and life is so sweet

I have glimpsed the future
and it is bright

In my children's, children's, children
I leave my legacy of hope

Look unto them
and see me

Through them
I am with you
always and forever

Weep not
for I
have been full circle

I have found peace

Author's notes: In loving memory of Debi's grandfather, Clarence Jacob. This was intended as simply a gift for her grandmother, but she requested this be read at his funeral.

Treasured Memories

Footprints

*The letter came
just the other day*

*Your struggle
I hadn't known*

*Strong, you were
... so full of life*

*The news
sent me reeling*

Why is it always the good ones?

*Years ago
you left a mark on my life*

*You ...
might never have realized
I ...
will never forget*

*Struggling
I was
but willing to try*

*An honest chance
... was all I asked*

*Somehow ...
you noticed*

*You
gave me that chance
... and so much more*

*You
gave me your friendship*

*You
made a difference
(...in this life anyway)*

~ ~ ~

*Footprints
we leave
in the lives of others*

*And what will ours be?
A mark
or a stain?*

Author's notes: In memory of David Lee Kelley

Songbird

*Silence
falls on the stage
broken only by the crickets*

*Winds soft magic
tickles the leaves*

*Soft spotlight
And you are there*

*Your voice
... beckons*

*Misty time
... evaporates*

*Sweet strains
... send me*

*Soul songs
poured from your heart
... take me
... steal me away*

*Ears
... drink in*

*Eyes
... all a'misty*

*The hemlocks
reverberate heaven*

Sweet mother music
such a debt we owe

You send your children
... your blessing
to play for us
... move us

to sing for our souls

My lady
how do we repay?

Author's notes: This poem was inspired by an outdoor concert given by a famous singer. The artist's name is not important, as this applies to all artists who give us the gift of music.

Mother Earth

*I wander my majestic distances
and weep*

*I have been raped
... torn asunder*

*And these children
who say they love their children
LIE
and leave them nothing*

Majestic Distances

Author's notes: This is a poem about Norwegian speed skater Johann Olav Koss, who raced in the 1994 Winter Olympics in Lillehammer, Norway. Koss had more-or-less adopted a young blind boy who was also physically challenged in other ways. Koss took the boy under his wing, and used to take him to all of his events. I have obviously taken some poetic license here, as Koss never said anything resembling these words about this particular race. This was drawn from seeing a television feature about his relationship with the boy, then watching the race itself. After putting up sparkling early split times, it seemed to me that Koss began to fade a bit. But then, Koss seemed to summon up something from deep within.

Echoes of Legends

The whistle
calls them to their marks

And an awesome hush ...
overwhelms the crowd

Then echoes of legends
race away with the gun

Yet the little one ...
only hears it
and feels it
As the skates ...
whistle and scrape by

The split times go up
and like a jet engine
The crowd ...
roars to life

The second split
and the engine is warming

The third
and its full ...
throaty voice is heard

The home town boy
is in the lead!

But for the hometown boy
The roar ...
melts into nothingness

I've poured everything
... everything
into this one

The Olympics ...

on my home turf
... chance of a lifetime
... just can't let them down

There's the bell
... last lap

... got two turns left
and the outside lane
I have ...
the lead

but I have
... nothing left

What do they say
'How's his last 400m?'

But another bell is ringing
A bell ...
rung by the little one

Certain things
this little one ...
cannot do

But this little one
... believes
that I ...
can do this thing

No - No
This is my turf
I do the last 400m

... better than anyone
I do this better
because ...

There is a little one
amongst the roar
who can't do everything
but he believes ...
that I ...
can do this thing

I hear ...
his cowbell alone

My frailties ...
immaterial
My fears ...
inconsequential

There is a little one
in those stands
who will learn today
that courage and love ...
conquers anything

Johann Olav Koss - World
Record / Gold Medal,
1500m Speed Skate

*Koss won two other Gold
Medals, also in World
Record time.*

Approaching Darkness

*To really live
is to experience
extremes*

*The darkness
approaches
us all*

*Know we,
this wondrous gift that is life
until death approaches?*

*Know we love,
until loneliness approaches?*

*All things ...
good and bad
are gifts from God*

*Some gifts
... just harder to see*

*Yet for all
- a rhyme
- a reason*

*Therefore
I fear not
your "darkness"*

I will take

this sputtering torch

*I will delve
the darkness*

*I will shine
my little light there*

*I will expose
the darkness*

*I will drag
her dark secrets
into the light*

*Yet tarry here
will I not*

*But come...
take my hand*

*I will lead you
into the light*

For Gale

That spark of life
That mini whirlwind
with eyes so full of question and wonder

Such trust you've found in those eyes
so pure
so real
... no strings

But life
is hard
The ugly
seeks the innocent

The little ones
also ride that great wheel of life

They too
must hang in the balances

But often we forget
An incredible gift has been given
and it is indeed a gift
... to be treasured

For time
is the only thing that is certain

other than those trusting eyes
... so pure
... so real

Never forget

*For this is the gift
above all others
however fleeting*

Author's notes: Written for an aunt whose son was diagnosed with leukemia. God was kind. Thankfully, Robbie has been in remission for many years now.

The Column and the Ivy

I am the column

My form
speaks of continuity

My presence
speaks of strength

My look
speaks of everlastings

Lean on me
for my one desire
is to stand
for you

I am the ivy

I am that special touch
that simple beauty

Clothing long, hard lines
with soft, gentle curves
... winding embraces of forever

Adorning strength
with completeness
... with fresh spring green

My gentle magic ...
speaks of everlastings

Author's notes: A portrait of marriage.

Stalwart Spires

Yesterday's Girl

Soft summer girl
of yesterday's life

Flowing cornsilk
and emeralds on fire

Lace and perfume
and endless clover kisses

A silky dream dance
on a stage
... long fallen silent

known only ...
to the wind

Author's notes: For my first true love.

Memories of Yesteryear

Searching for the River

Being together
... so empty

The plans
... never kept

The promises
... always broken

But being apart
... so lonely

Yet we fight for our "rights"
... for what is "ours"

Never knowing
we fight the wrong battle

Never seeing
that we only fight ourselves

Yet in the misty distance
courses a river
A river of harmony and peace

A few have sighted it
but no one has found it
no one ever really arrives

Still its strength nurtures many

For strength
comes not from the finding

Strength

is found in the search

*For when two will
to search together*

Peace will come

*Harmony's gentle waters
will lap laughingly at your feet*

Still Yourself

Part 1
The Yard

Quieting down
it is ...
Long light
streams through the trees
The grill
slowly dies down

And soon, the stars ...
the delicious cool of the evening

And I still myself
... and listen
to misty echoes
of times past in this yard

The squeals of laughter
around that wading pool
... couldn't get grass to grow there for months

The peculiar rolling thunder
of Bigwheel races around the yard

The shrieks
when that bungle bee (sic)
got caught in your hair.

... allergic to stings
I pulled it out with my hand

And the parties
Cold libations
Steaks and "Dave's famous brats" on the grill
The volleyball games
... tore up my knee that night

That swing
... took longer than I thought to build

But there's just something about a swing
that gentle motion in the moonlight
enjoyed by lovers and friends alike

The effort
all worth it
... needs refinishing now

Still yourself
... listen

The earth
She will speak to you

Part 2
Colorado

The mountains ...
blow you away

But the ghost town of
St. Elmo
takes you back

You remember the road up
and you wonder how they
managed it

Then they tell you
that the silver bars
were stacked up like
cordwood.

But that day has gone
in more ways than one
Now they tell me
it has burned to the ground

But I can look at the
pictures
and remember the
peacefulness

I can still myself
and listen
to the bustle of the past

The fortunes

... risked
... won
and lost

Still yourself ...
in these places
and you will hear it

Part 3
Waswagoning

Authentic Ojibwe village
re-creations
Guided tours
... so said the sign

So we paid our money
expecting the standard
tourist clap-trap

But as he spoke to me
I looked in his eyes
... and I saw it
This Ojibwe man
who said he knew a little
medicine
He could hear the echoes
of distant times

This was the summer camp
... the time of plenty
Tribes could now come
together
(over)

because of the abundance

The men tussled and competed
... testing their strength
and played lacrosse games
that ranged for square miles

His Dakota wife
told of the women
who were romanced by these lakes
with the long light of the moon
stretching her silvery
fingers across the waters
... to soften young hearts

And she tells me
of the winter camp
... of the hardship
... of the passing

He tells me
of the weapons camp
of the careful crafting
A bad arrow...
and you went hungry
or died in battle

And she tells me
of the communion
between spirit ...
earth ...

and man

Of the pain
of leaving your land
... of the trail of tears

One sixty-forth Cherokee
... I am
... almost too little to claim

But I was still
and I listened

... and something awoke

Part 4
Echoes Past

I slip back to the present
and the yard

And I listen to the earth
... anew

Here ...
worlds collided

A Native American warrior
fought a bear here
... and won

A young brave
souyhl his vision here

... to be a peacemaker

A tribe
made its camp here
... with hunting parties
leaving with the dawn
returning at dusk
laden with their successes

... Happy hours shared
in the magic of the firelight

But soon ...
Conestoga wagons roll
through
Soon followed
by horse soldiers

I still myself
and listen ...
and hear the truth

We came ...
to save their souls
But they already knew
the Great Creator

We came ...
to educate them
But they lived here
for thousands of years
and never left a mark

We have lived here
for just a few hundred
and have destroyed
the place

Exactly what was it
that they did not know?

The truth is
we sought our fortunes here
our silvery Colorado
dreams
But "savages"
stood in our way

So our horse soldier
"heroes"
ruthlessly slaughtered here

My kindred ...
were dispossessed here
My kindred ...
fell here

The earth ...
cries out with their blood

There is much
I have not heard
I must learn to listen
more closely

Still yourself
...listen to Mother Earth

And she will speak to you.

Grandfather Mandela

It is his birthday ...
and he wants a toy

So you bring him there
but they are there too

He holds your left hand
While the throngs ...
grasp your right

You are his grandfather
and their grandfather

You are ...
grandfather ...
to a nation

He could never know

Twenty-seven years ...
on Robien Island
with only books ...
and hope ...
and a garden ...
to sustain you

A heavy price was paid ...
to set a nation free

The cost...
he could never know
... could never fathom

"Grandpa, let me hold your right hand
... so they cannot"

*Grandfather must choose
between child
and nation*

*He chooses wisely
he chooses nation*

*After many hours
the throngs finally leave*

*But the little one tired
many hours ago
and no longer wants his toy*

Oh, little man ...

*Some day
you will come to know
... the sacrifice
... the price*

*And you will be proud
... unto tears
just to be able to say*

*I held his left hand
while in his right ...
he held a nation*

Author's notes: President Nelson Mandela told this story about a time when he took his grandson to the store to buy him a toy. People instantly recognized him, and throngs of people mobbed him, just wanting to shake his hand. He held his grandson with his left hand and shook hands with his right. Anxious for his toy, the boy kept asking grandpa to hold his right hand so he wouldn't be able to shake hands with any more of the crowd.

Author's notes: This poem still leaves me scratching my head, and I'm the one who wrote it!
This was supposed to be a wedding poem for my niece Barb, but what tumbled out was this fairy tale. When they first met, her husband Kidi swore to her, "I like you a lot, but I'll never love you." Well, her feminine charms saw to that! He is from Finland, thus, I give you ...

The Ice Prince

Alone
in distant halls
of hoar frost
dwelt the ice prince

Sworn never to love
he sat aloof
on his throne of blue ice
his halls
and his heart
long shuttered to the light

Once
the legends say
these halls
glistened with wealth

But those days had passed
and the ice had come
Blue ice walls
now echoed with emptiness
His icy throne
seemed to hold him in sway

Then one day
chance brought
a knock on his door

Strangers ...
were usually sent away
But a storm raged
and somehow
this maiden
... adorned in green
slipped over his threshold

Just a girl
he thought
Quite fair
but just a girl

But then
she smiled

Just a smile
... it was
But ah ...
what a smile

Pure sunshine
... it was

It's warm radiance
refracted in the blue ice
filling his halls
with shimmering ...

crystalline ...
rainbow magic

Entranced
he begged her to tarry
And as they spoke
Slowly ...
subtly ...
his halls
and his heart
began to warm

But soon the storm passed
and she left
but with a promise to
return

And quickly
the chill
... the emptiness
returned to his halls

The maiden
and her smile
would return

But never ...
was it soon enough
Never ...
was it long enough

Sworn never to love
he began to secretly long
for the light of her smile

Somewhere

deep inside him
a little flame
had leapt to life

making the cold
seem crueler
making the loneliness
seem emptier

Then one day
as the maiden departed
he ventured a question

"Should I ever seek you,
where would I find you?"

She smiled
and quietly spoke

"These halls ...
hide a secret,
as too ...
does your heart

Find those secrets
and you ...
will find me"

And quickly
she was gone

The cold crept back quickly
as did the emptiness
... the secret yearning

Longer and longer
would she be absent
(over)

*And deeper
would the silence
… the emptiness
echo through his frostbitten
halls
As too …
did her words
echo …
through the empty halls of
his heart*

*Till one day his heart
could bear it no more
No longer
could he hide
that flame in his heart*

*The secret she spoke of
he would find
… come what may*

*His great sword was drawn
and heavy blows fell
on the throne of blue ice
that had held him in sway*

*The ice fell away
and beneath
lay a throne of pure gold*

*In wonder …
he gazed at it
Then within it
his reflection he saw*

He stared

in amazement

*This was not the cold
sad visage
he had seen in the ice
It was a visage of warmth …
of wholeness …
of light …
of love*

*Instantly
he knew
he had found the secret*

*Then as if by strange magic
came that knock on his
door*

*And once again
that smile
slipped over his threshold*

*Instantly he knew
what he must do*

*He leapt to the windows
and threw back the
shutters*

*Soon sunlight was
streaming
o'er hearth and heart
string*

*And then she smiled
and ah …*

what a smile

* * *

At first ...
it was faint
... soft cracking
then the patter of dripping

But the frost could not hide
from love's glowing
radiance
Soon his halls were alive
with the sound of the
melting

Sparkling cascades
now tumbled down
in shimmering ...
crystalline ...
rainbow magic
revealing the secret
long hidden beneath

The blue ice had hidden
halls burnished in gold

Too long
had the hoar frost
hidden it's brilliance

Only now
could her sunshine
reveal it's true magic
Only now
could his heart
feel love ...

too long hidden

Gently
he took her hand
and on deep bended knee
said,

"M' lady,
Too long ...
has the frost
held sway in my life
Too long
have I hidden
this flame in my heart

I have swung wide
these shutters
... in my halls
... in my heart

I have let
love's light in

Come, fair maiden
dwell with me
... in halls
now of gold

Ever ...
will we walk
in the sunshine

Ever ...
will we dwell
in love's light"

www.ingramcontent.com/pod-product-compliance
Lightning Source LLC
Chambersburg PA
CBHW041431300426
44116CB00001B/5